PUFFIN BOOKS
EEKS! I SAW AN ANT!

Arthy Muthanna Singh is a children's writer, freelance journalist, copywriter, editor and cartoonist. She has authored more than thirty-five books for children. Currently, she is a partner at Syllables27, an outfit that produces books for children on a turnkey basis for publishers and organizations that work with children.

Mamta Nainy is a children's writer, editor and translator based in New Delhi, whose book *A Brush with Indian Art* won The Hindu Young World–Goodbooks Award 2019 for Best Book (Non-Fiction).

Priyankar Gupta is an animation film designer and an illustrator from National Institute of Design. He has also been working as a pre-visualizer for television commercials and feature films. He is a visiting faculty and mentor in various design institutes across the country.

About the Series

It's time to enter the fascinating
kingdom of insects with WWF India's
EEKS series! From bees to flies, from ants to
wasps and from mosquitoes to cockroaches, the
books in this unique series will introduce you to
a vast variety of insects we share our planet with
and help you discover some jaw-dropping facts
about them. So, what are you waiting for?
Bug out, have fun and be prepared
to be amazed!

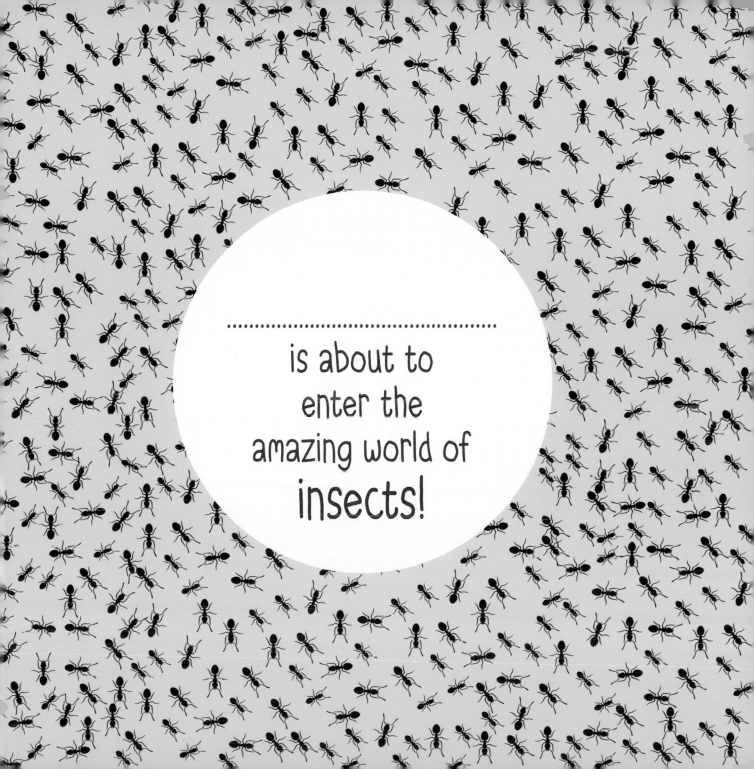

....

is about to
enter the
amazing world of
insects!

PUFFIN BOOKS

USA | Canada | UK | Ireland | Australia
New Zealand | India | South Africa | China

Puffin Books is part of the Penguin Random House group of companies
whose addresses can be found at global.penguinrandomhouse.com

Published by Penguin Random House India Pvt. Ltd
No: 04-010 to 04-012, 4th Floor, Capital Tower -1,
M G Road, Gurugram -122002, Haryana, India

Penguin
Random House
India

First published in Puffin Books by Penguin Random House India 2021

Text and illustrations copyright © World Wide Fund for Nature-India 2021

ISBN 9780143450993

Layout and design by Aniruddha Mukherjee
Typeset in Bembo Infant by Syllables27, New Delhi
Printed at Aarvee Promotions, India

www.penguin.co.in

EEEEEEKKKS!

I SAW AN ANT!

Arthy Muthanna Singh and Mamta Nainy

Illustrations by Priyankar Gupta

PUFFIN BOOKS

An imprint of Penguin Random House

EEEEEEKKKS!

Ants are good but can be a bit bad,

When they bite, it is a little sad.

They work so hard, watch and see,

With six frantic legs, off they scurry.

Don't leave honey, near and far,

Or yummy jelly in an open jar . . .

Ants will be there right away,

Any time of the night or day!

What are the four words you think of when you see an ant?

1. ....

2. ....

3. ....

4. ....

BOO!

Did you know that the fear of ants is called myrmecophobia (mer-me-co-pho-bia)?

2

FOLLOW THE
ANTS!

1 , 2, 3, 4, 5, 6, 7, 8, 9, 10 . . . 99 . . .' Mona was counting out loud. 'What are you doing?' asked her father sleepily. He was lying on the grass in the garden after playing cricket with Mona for two hours.

'Don't move, Papa!' said Mona, 'I am counting the ants that are walking over you.'

'Walking over me?' asked Papa.

'Yes. They are all carrying something,' said Mona. 'Small bits of the biscuit I dropped this morning.'

After two minutes, Papa asked, 'Can I turn over now?'

'Yes, you can. The last ant in the line has crossed your back,' said Mona. 'Come, Papa, let us follow the ants. I want to know where they are going.'

'They must be going for their Physical Training (PT) class!' said Papa, turning over and smiling.

'Papa!' Mona exclaimed. 'Be serious. Nobody goes for PT class with bits of biscuit in their mouths!'

So Mona and Papa crawled behind the straight line of ants across the green lawn and through the flower beds. They finally reached a brick wall at the end of the garden. As the two watched, all the ants disappeared one by one into a tiny hole between two bricks.

Just then, Mina, Mona's mother, looked out of her bedroom window. She saw them still on their knees, staring keenly at something.

'What are you two doing?' she called out.

'Following the ants, Mama!' said Mona, and she and her father started laughing.

ANTS ARE AMAZING!

Have you ever noticed a string of small dashes on a wall? But when you look closer, you find the dashes moving, and then you figure out that each dash is actually an ant walking in a line, one behind the other, till you discover an entire army of ants marching down the wall to a corner where lies a tiny crumb of bread!

Ants, like humans, are social creatures. They live in big colonies, which may contain a few to 20 million ants! Many ant colonies spread over a large area also unite to form a super colony. Ants can be found in every place on Earth, except Antarctica and a few remote islands. The reason they've been able to live comfortably almost anywhere is that ants can organize themselves very well.

ANT CITIES

In 2002, the largest recorded continuous colony of ants was found from northern Italy to the Atlantic coast of Spain. Stretching for 6000 km, it is made by the species of Argentine ant.

Soldier Ant

There are three types or castes of ants in an ant colony: the queen, the female workers and the drones (the males). The queen and the drones have wings, while the workers don't. A colony may have one or more than one queen. The wingless worker and soldier ants, who're often called the major workers, are female. They protect the queen, defend the colony, gather food and attack enemy colonies in search of food and nesting space. Most ant colonies also have some drones whose only job is to mate with the queen ant. They die soon after their job is done. In most cases, only the queen ant lays eggs. An ant colony is described as a superorganism because all the ants work together to support the colony. Doesn't that sound like a good housing society?

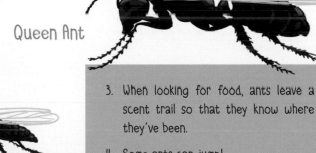

Queen Ant

Drone

Worker Ant

1. Queen ants can be incredibly long-lived. Some queen ants can live for many years and have millions of babies.

2. Ants don't have ears. They 'hear' by feeling vibrations in the ground through their feet.

3. When looking for food, ants leave a scent trail so that they know where they've been.

4. Some ants can jump!

5. Fire ants, a species of ants, have a unique way to avoid danger—they play dead when captured!

6. Certain species of ants raid other ant colonies, capture their workers and tame them to increase the workforce of their own colony.

TUNNELLING THROUGH TIME

Ants have been on this planet for at least 100 million years—far outlasting the dinosaurs! Myrmecologists or scientists who specialize in the study of ants have found that ants are related to wasps and bees. But while all species of ants are social and live in groups, their cousins, wasps, are mainly known to be solitary insects who lead single lives.

There are more than 10,000 species of ants all over the world. The sizes of ants vary from 0.075 cm to 5.2 cm. Among the largest ants in the world are the giant Amazonian ants of the genus *Dinoponera* from South America, which measure around 3–4 cm. From fossils found in Messel, Germany, scientists have found out that around 50 million years ago, queens of a unique species of ants lived in Europe, which were 6 cm long and had a wingspan of 15 cm. You must have seen ants that are red or black, but they can be brown, green or yellow too. Some of them bite, of course! But overall, compared to some other insects, most ants are pretty harmless.

LOOK CLOSELY!

Like other insects, ants have a head, thorax and abdomen. If you carefully observe an ant's head, the antennae are always moving—touching, tasting and smelling everything the ant can reach. Each antenna is bent in the middle like the elbow of your arm. Mandibles are an important part of an ant. They are the ant's jaws. Ants use their mandibles for biting, crushing, cutting, digging, fighting and hunting. They use them like we use our hands to hold and carry things. Ants also have compound eyes with hundreds of lenses that create a single image in the brain. Cool, right?

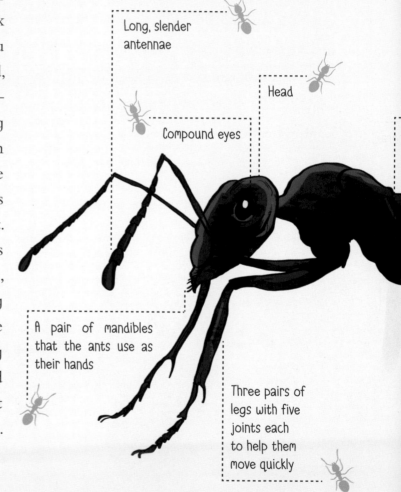

Long, slender antennae

Head

Compound eyes

A pair of mandibles that the ants use as their hands

Three pairs of legs with five joints each to help them move quickly

9

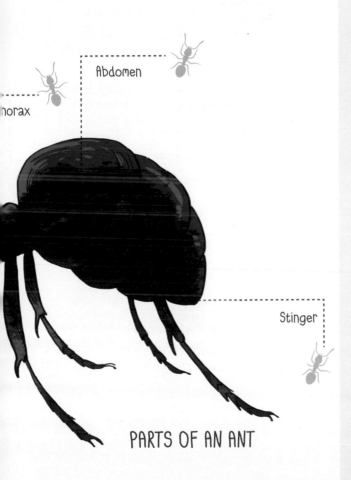

Abdomen

Thorax

Stinger

PARTS OF AN ANT

BET YOU DIDN'T KNOW THIS!

One of the most amazing insects on the planet, ants can lift heavy weights, coordinate with each other and some can even swim. Impressed with these creatures, James McLurkin, an assistant professor at Rice University, USA, created robots that behaved like ants. These robots have small internal computers that help them communicate with each other, similar to a colony of ants. They can help with exploration, search and rescue operations and mapping.

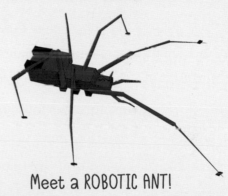

Meet a ROBOTIC ANT!

EXOSKELETON

Ants, like all insects, are invertebrates —meaning they do not have a backbone. They have a hard covering called an exoskeleton on the outside of their bodies.

IT'S AN ANT'S LIFE!

Unlike some insects who live only for a few days or even a few hours, ants, especially queen ants of one particular species called the western harvester ants, can live for decades! Most worker ants, however, live from one to three years and drones, poor things, only for a few weeks!

The life cycle of the ant includes four stages—egg, larva, pupa and adult. After a spell of hot summer rain, a young queen ant flies out of the ant colony in search of mates. The queen ant releases chemical substances called pheromones to attract males. The female then builds a nest and colony of her own and starts laying eggs, most of which hatch into workers. During the next few months, the ants develop through the four stages, thereby going through a metamorphosis—a complete change. A new worker ant spends the first few days of its adult life caring for the queen and the young. It then moves on to do digging and other nest work, and later to defending the nest and searching for food outside the colony. It is similar to going from Class 1 to Class 2 to Class 3 . . .

SHOW ME THE WAY!

Ants 'talk' to each other using pheromones, sounds and touch. Like other insects, ants can detect smells with their long antennae. Since most ants live on the ground, they leave pheromone trails that may be followed by other ants. For example, if one ant finds food, it will mark a trail on the way back to the colony, which the other ants will follow. They will walk in a line while being led by the scent of the leader and eventually reach where the food is. Ants are active all-year round in warm places, but they hibernate in the winter in cold places.

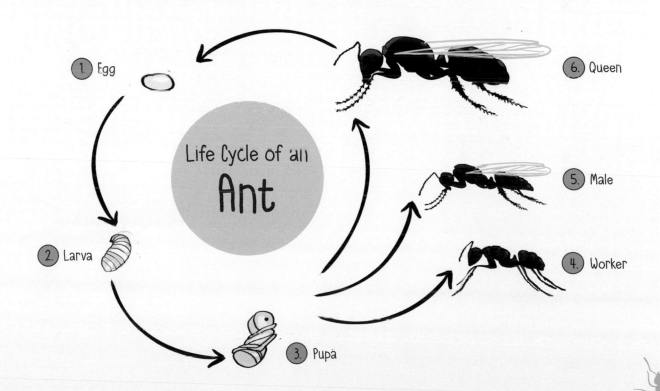

Ants are like us in so many ways! Some ants grow their own crops of fungus, similar to humans farming mushrooms. Some build colonies like professional builders. Some weave beautiful nests like master weavers. While some others are courageous warriors who go to war with other ants. But like some of us, some ants are very clever too! Like robber or thief ants, who nest close to other ant nests and steal their food, or slave-making ants, who capture broods of other ant colonies so as to increase the workforce of their colonies! Let's look at some of the most amazingly strange ants in the ant world.

DRACULA ANTS

Found in the tropical regions of Asia and Africa, dracula ants live underground or in deep leaf litter and are rarely seen. These ants are fierce predators. They catch tiny insects and chow them down—they're the vampires of the ant world! They can strike a whopping 5000 times faster than the blink of an eye—they're known to have recorded the single fastest animal movement ever observed. Ready, steady . . . chomp!

1.5 mm (*Mystrium camillae*)

HERDER ANTS

Like humans domesticate cows for their milk, herder ants have their own farms and domesticate tiny insects like aphids. The aphids eat plant sap and produce a clear, sugary substance, or 'milk', that the herder ants love. The chemicals on ants' feet also sedate aphid colonies, keeping them close by as a ready source of food.

5-7 mm (*Dolichoderus cuspidatus*)

BULLET ANTS

Bullet ants are said to have the most painful sting in the world. Living in humid conditions such as the Amazon jungle, their sting, which lasts 12–24 hours, has been compared to being hit by a bullet.

25 mm (*Paraponera clavata*)

EXPLODING ANTS

Exploding ants are the suicide bombers of the ant world! Found in Malaysia, these tiny brownish-red ants take their job as soldiers very seriously. Their insides are full of poisonous sacks. When a predator appears, they contract their muscles to build up the poison. And then, similar to a pressure cooker, they explode, spraying the toxins on the predator.

6-12 mm (*Colobopsis explodens*)

ANTS, ANTS EVERYWHERE!

Tunnelling out of jungles and forests and wandering into backyards, ants can be found almost everywhere. They creep, they crawl, they climb and they fall. But they get up and keep going.

In India, we can find around 828 ant species, out of which 256 are endemic. Below are some of the major groups of ants.

HARVESTER ANTS

Like the name tells you, these ants harvest seeds of different types of grasses. You can easily spot them in a garden, park or lawn where they create corridors or passages. These ants move one behind the other. They bring grass seeds and store them in neat granaries. Very smartly, the harvester ants remove the shoots of the seeds so that the seeds do not germinate in their nests. The seeds can then be stored as food for a long time, ensuring no ant starves!

5-7 mm (*Pheidologeton diversus*)

WEAVER ANTS

These ants weave beautiful, football-sized nests with leaves. Resembling a piece of art, these nests can be seen on mango, citrus and guava trees, if you look very carefully. Worker ants fold the leaves and join them with glue that is secreted by the larvae. This glue is known as silk. The reddish-brown ants protect the fruits of the tree that these nests are built on from other pests, making sure that 'their' host tree is taken care of. Really sweet, is it not?

4-11 mm (*Oecophylla smaragdina*)

LEAFCUTTER ANTS

Leafcutter ants cultivate fungi in their nests. They bring fresh leaves and plant cuttings into their nests, which they cut into smaller and smaller pieces and cover with their faecal liquid. Ecks! Then these are placed in the part of the nest where the fungus is cultivated. The ants begin to feed on the fungus, which is rich in carbohydrates and proteins.

2-14 mm (*Atta sexdens*)

ARMY ANTS

They are called army ants probably because they move so well, just like the army! These ants move during the day, capturing small insects to feed their brood, and at dusk, they form their nests, which they change almost daily. They are also great predators and even large prey, like scorpions, cannot escape the clutches of these ants.

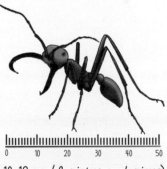

10-12 mm (*Aenictus ceylonicus*)

TINY BUT MIGHTY

Did you know that ants are one of the strongest creatures on Earth? They have a talent for weightlifting and, depending on the species, a single ant can carry twenty to 100 times its own body weight. Interestingly, an elephant can lift a log that is about one-fifth its body weight. Ants even work together to move bigger objects as a group!

But how do ants manage to move so easily and quickly with objects that are so much heavier than their body mass? Well, while humans rely on hefty back muscles and elephants use their trunks, ants depend on their mandibles for the real heavy lifting. Some ants like the trap-jaw ants have such powerful muscles in their mandibles that if they strike their mandibles against the ground and snap them shut, they can even launch themselves into the air, somersaulting several times like a master gymnast!

Ants move their legs in two groups of three. The front and back legs on the left side of the ant and the middle leg on the right side move together and touch the ground, while the other three legs swing forward. And then, the front and back legs on the right side and the middle leg on the left side touch the ground, while the rest are moving. Even while running, ants always keep at least three legs on the ground. So, faster and faster they go . . .

Ants can also change the size and shape of the pads on their feet depending on the load they are carrying. If they have to carry heavy loads, they increase the contact area, and when they need to run, they decrease it. The pads on ants' feet are self-cleaning and can stick to almost any type of surface—no man-made glue can match this!

WHAT'S ON THE MENU?

Ants will eat practically any kind of food: other ants, dead insects, parts of dead animals, grains, fruits and vegetables, but they are especially attracted to sweets. We all know that, don't we? Being the social insects that they are, whenever they find food, they carry it back to the colony to share. Ants exchange food with other ants using their mouths—a way to share nutrition and chemicals and of saying 'we're a family!'

19

Cats, dogs and other pets can invite ants into your home. Their food and water bowls are very tempting for ants! So keep pet bowls clean and get rid of any spilled food or water right away. Store dry pet food in a sealed container instead of paper bags, which ants can easily enter. Remember that ants can fit through even the tiniest openings!

ANTING

Did you know that a large number of birds indulge in anting—an activity in which they crush ants and rub them all over their plumage?

The formic acid released from the ants helps to keep parasites away!

ANTS ARE AWESOME!

Ants are one of the world's most important insects. They are major soil turners, pollinators, scavengers, biological control agents . . . and they do it all absolutely free of charge! Let's find out the many good things that ants do.

1. The ants that live in soil dig tunnels that provide holes for air and water. They often turn over more soil a year than earthworms, which results in more underground passageways for plant roots. This leads to the gaseous exchange between plants and the soil.

2. Ants are the garbage collectors of soil. The species that nest in the ground break down organic matter—dead leaves, stems, roots or food scraps—and improve the soil's quality. The soil is richer and looser and, most importantly, it soaks in water better.

3. Ants are an important part of the food chain—many ant species prey on other insects and pests like termites. They also provide food for many animals and birds (and even carnivorous plants like the pitcher plant)!

4. Some ants, such as weaver ants, help in citrus cultivation. Weaver ants feed on insects like the citrus stink bug, leaf-feeding caterpillars, aphids and the citrus leaf miner, which attack orange, tangerine, lemon and pomelo trees and their fruits. Use of the weaver ant as a pest management method protects the fruits from pests.

5. Some ants are of medical importance. The salivary secretions of ants are believed to have antibiotic properties. In ancient cultures, the venom of the black samsum ant, commonly found in Saudi Arabia, was used to treat a host of illnesses such as inflammation, body ache and hepatitis.

6. Some ants have a special relationship with the rare alcon blue butterfly that lays its eggs on a plant called the marsh gentian. First the caterpillar feeds on this plant and then it drops to the ground. If it's lucky, it's picked up by a particular kind of red ant. Since the caterpillar resembles the queen, the worker ants carefully carry the caterpillar back to its nest where they look after it till the adult butterfly crawls out of the ant nest and flies away. That is definitely the behaviour of a friend in need, don't you think?

ANT HANG-OUTS!

Ants generally occupy a variety of habitats such as leaf litter, trees, soil and dead logs, while there are also tramp ants that prefer human-modified habitats.

Here are some of the types of nests that ants make:

1. Nests in the soil
2. Mound nests
3. Rotting logs
4. Nests in tree bases
5. Nests in concrete structures
6. Arboreal nests

Some ants are nomads and are always on the move. So they bunch together to ensure the protection of the queen as she moves in the centre.

Kitchens are places where ants can snack on food all day long. So they are naturally drawn to kitchens. Bathrooms, bedrooms, living rooms, basements, inside walls and the area in or around air conditioners also attract ants.

The easiest way to avoid sharing your home with an ant colony is to keep it tidy. Wipe kitchen counters clean and sweep floors regularly to remove food crumbs. Store food in sealed containers, and keep ripe fruit in the refrigerator. Wipe sticky jars, especially any with honey, syrup, soda or other sweets. Finally, use a lid on trash cans and get rid of garbage regularly. Repair leaky pipes, and check under sinks for areas of moisture.

ANTS AND HERBAL TEA

In South Africa, ants are used to help harvest the seeds of rooibos, a plant used to make herbal tea. The plant disperses its seeds widely, making manual collection difficult. Black ants collect and store these seeds in their nests, where humans can gather them. Up to 200 g of seeds can be collected from one ant heap!

ANTS UP CLOSE

WHAT ANTS LIKE AND WHAT THEY DON'T

LIKE	DON'T LIKE
Honeydew	Vinegar and lime juice
Sugar or crumbs lying on the floor or on the kitchen top	Chalk
Fungus	Beetles, fish, lizards, sparrows and snakes who eat them
Dead insects	Pesticides
Picnics	Cemented courtyards
Gardens, hedges, fields and forests	Herbs such as peppermint, sage, spearmint, thyme, etc., which keep ants away

NATURE'S AMAZING CREW

Now you know that ants have many great lessons to teach us about family, teamwork and the importance of ecology or the environment. They are small in size, but mighty when it comes to hard work and resourcefulness. So watch where you step, these important members of nature's crew might be marching underfoot!

LAUGH OUT LOUD!

Which is the biggest ant in the world?

An eleph-ant!

TURTLE ANT

When a turtle ant falls, it has a unique ability to 'parachute' and steer its fall so as to land back on the tree trunk rather than fall to the ground. It also uses its unique disc-like head to plug the entrance to its nest to prevent enemies from gaining access.

So ants don't really deserve an EEKS, do they? Now, write four things that you think are amazing about ants.

1. ....

2. ....

3. ....

4. ....

T. REX ANT

In 2003, an entomologist in Malaysia found a single dead ant whose little mandibles reminded him of *Tyrannosaurus rex*'s mini arms. And so, he named the new species *Tyrannomyrmex rex*. Surprisingly, unlike their namesake, these ants are said to be quite timid.

SOME FUN WORDS TO KNOW ABOUT ANTS

1. **Anthill:** The nest that ants build out of dirt or sand that looks like a mini hill.
2. **Ant farm:** An enclosed structure for the study of ant colonies and how ants behave.
3. **Alate:** Winged queen and drone ants.
4. **Ergate:** Worker ant.
5. **Dinergate:** Soldier ant.
6. **Myrmecologists:** Those who study ants.

Did you know?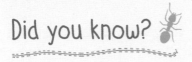

1. Queen ants shed their wings when they start a new nest.

2. Ants don't have lungs. They have tiny holes called spiracles all over their body through which they breathe in oxygen and release carbon dioxide.

3. When the queen ant dies, the colony can only survive a few months. Queens are rarely replaced and the workers are not able to reproduce. But in some species, the death of the queen might trigger a 'laying worker' phenomenon, where the worker ants start producing eggs.

4. Ants have jaws that open and shut sideways almost like a pair of scissors.

5. Ants have compound eyes. They contain hundreds of lenses that combine to form a single image in the ant's brain. They also have three small simple eyes on the top of the head called ocelli that detect light levels.

Activity 1

Apart from ants, which other insect makes you say EEKS?

Draw and colour it.

Activity 2

Think of a new species of ant and name it. Now draw it in the box below.

Try it; it'll be fun!

Be a critter spotter!

Our backyards are filled with small fascinating creatures. Go outside and explore the world of insects. Make notes of all the insects that you spot—their sizes, shapes and colours. To help with the exploration, carry a magnifying glass. Make sure you take time to observe. Take photos of the bugs you see or draw their pictures. Write down which bugs you see and where you saw them. From watching a centipede dig in the soil to seeing a bee interact with a flower, there is no limit to the number of things you can discover. But do remember that you're like a giant for a teeny bug—they might get scared of you! Watch them, but don't touch them or pick them up.

More reading on insects

https://kids.nationalgeographic.com/animals/invertebrates/insects/

https://www.si.edu/spotlight/buginfo/incredbugs

https://theconversation.com/birds-bees-and-bugs-your-garden-is-an-ecosystem-and-it-needs-looking-after-65226

https://www.coolkidfacts.com/insect-facts/

https://kids.britannica.com/

Insect Identification Sheet

Date: ....   Time: ....

Draw the insect

Habitat of the insect

Describe where they are generally
found in the world

1. How many legs does the insect have?

2. Does the insect have wings?

3. Can you see its eyes?

4. What colour is it?

5. How many body parts does it have?

6. Does it fly, hop or crawl?

Name of the insect: ....

Acknowledgements

We owe a debt of gratitude to the people mentioned below.

Radhika Suri, for showing faith in us, serving as a sounding board for our ideas and navigating our course through the development of this series.

Sohini Mitra, for giving the EEKS series another home.

Shalini Agrawal and Aditi Batra for their editorial finesse.

Aniruddha Dhamorikar, Kaustubh Srikanth, Chetna Singh Kaith, Payal Narain and Surbhi Bhadani for their time, expertise and invaluable inputs.

Our wonderful illustrators—Aniruddha Mukherjee, Priyankar Gupta, Charulata Mukherjee and Mistunee Chowdhury—for sharing our enthusiasm and breathing life into the books with their wonderful illustrations.

And, of course, you, dear reader, for reading this book—we hope you enjoy reading these books as much as we did putting them together!

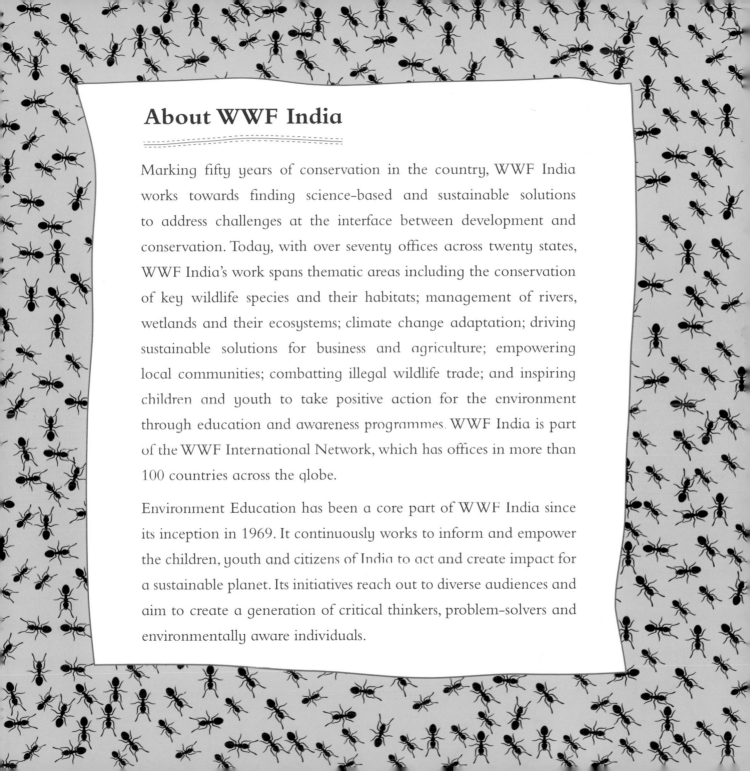

About WWF India

Marking fifty years of conservation in the country, WWF India works towards finding science-based and sustainable solutions to address challenges at the interface between development and conservation. Today, with over seventy offices across twenty states, WWF India's work spans thematic areas including the conservation of key wildlife species and their habitats; management of rivers, wetlands and their ecosystems; climate change adaptation; driving sustainable solutions for business and agriculture; empowering local communities; combatting illegal wildlife trade; and inspiring children and youth to take positive action for the environment through education and awareness programmes. WWF India is part of the WWF International Network, which has offices in more than 100 countries across the globe.

Environment Education has been a core part of WWF India since its inception in 1969. It continuously works to inform and empower the children, youth and citizens of India to act and create impact for a sustainable planet. Its initiatives reach out to diverse audiences and aim to create a generation of critical thinkers, problem-solvers and environmentally aware individuals.

Read More in the Series

  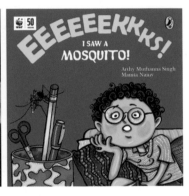

What's the buzz about bees? What do they do all day? Why are they important? Find out everything about bees in this buzzing book and discover the big ways in which these little insects contribute to our environment.

Whether cockroaches fill you with dread or wide-eyed wonder, there's no denying the fact that they are some of the most amazing creatures of the insect universe. So, dash right into their wonderful world, find out everything about them and be prepared to be super surprised!

Mosquitoes are mostly known as tiny troublemakers. But there are lots of interesting facts about these delicate insects. Read this book to find out about their many species, sizes, diets, homes and—most importantly—why they bite!